It's A Zoo In Here

Copyright 2022 © Gabriella Fabiano All rights reserved. This book or the original title "It's A Zoo In Here" or parts thereof may not be reproduced, photocopied, translated, stored in a database, or distributed in any form or by any means (electronic, optical, or mechanical, including photocopying or recording), without the express written and signed consent of the author.

Illustrations enhancement, Format, Cover, and Interior layout designed by Sunil Nissanka (Top rated freelancer on Upwork.com)
Contact: sumudamar@gmail.com

Today my family and I are going
to the zoo, woohoo!
Through the gates my family flew,
we were so excited we did not know
what to do!

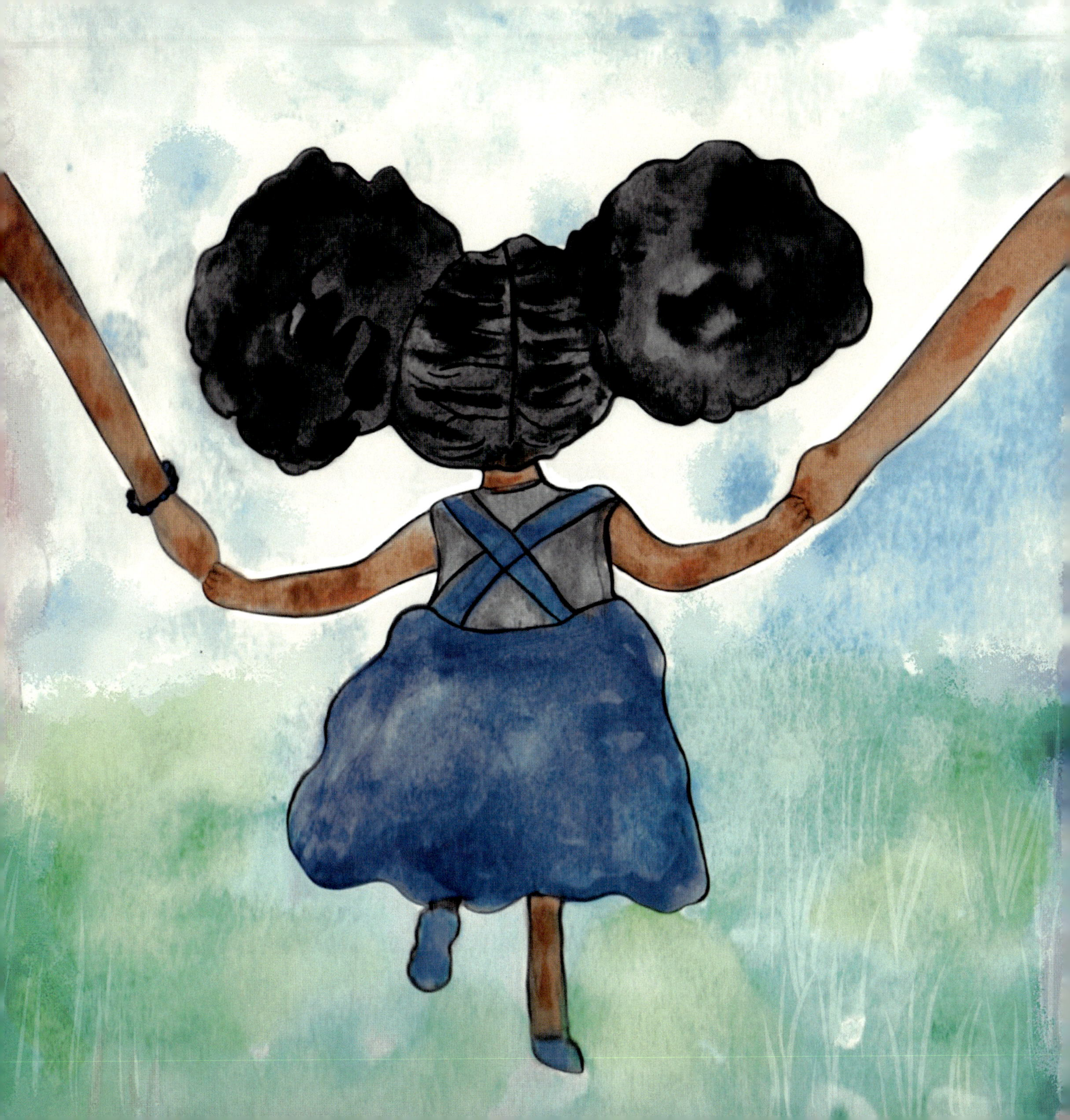

Elephant, we will start with you.

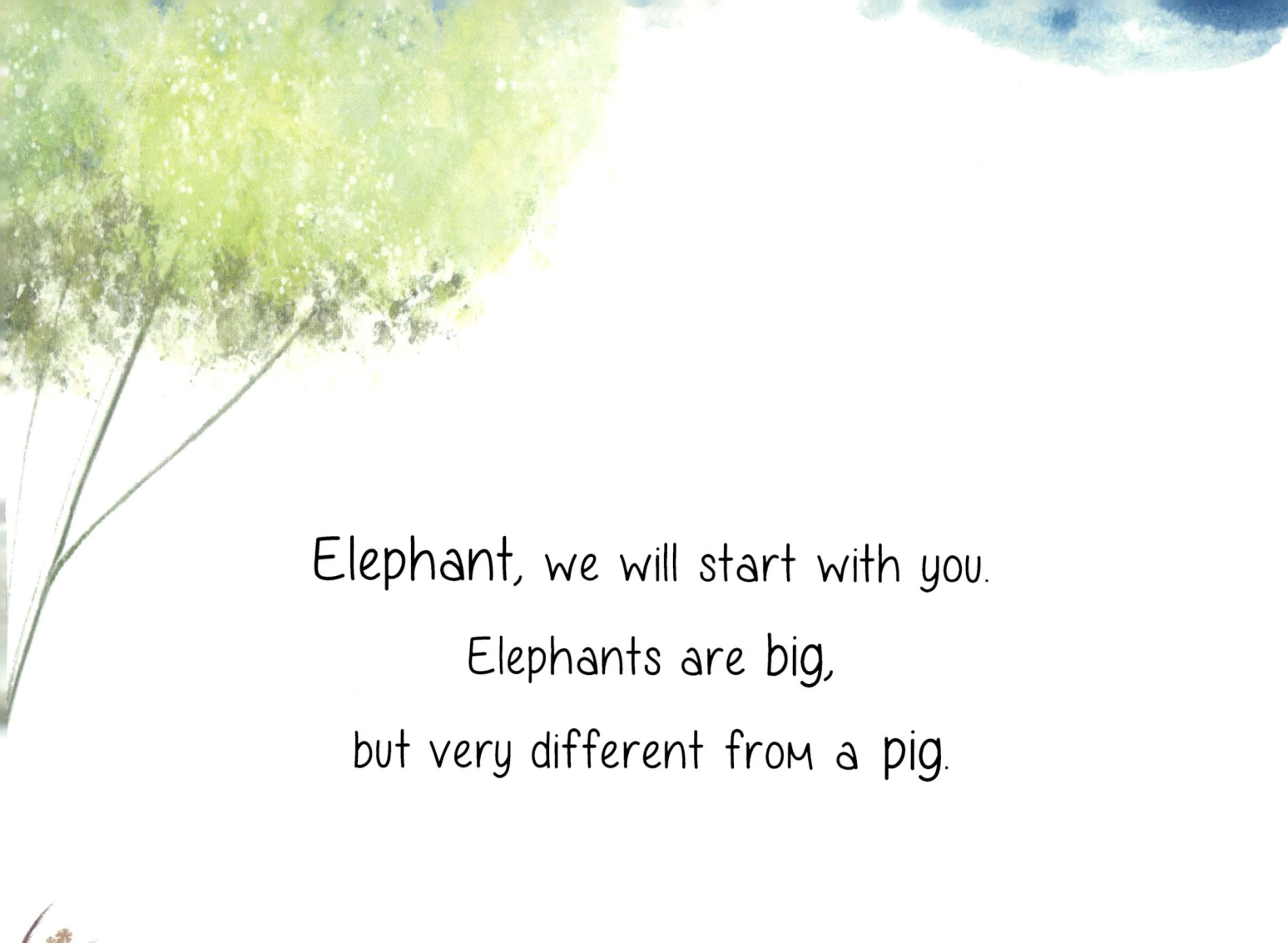

Elephants are big,

but very different from a pig.

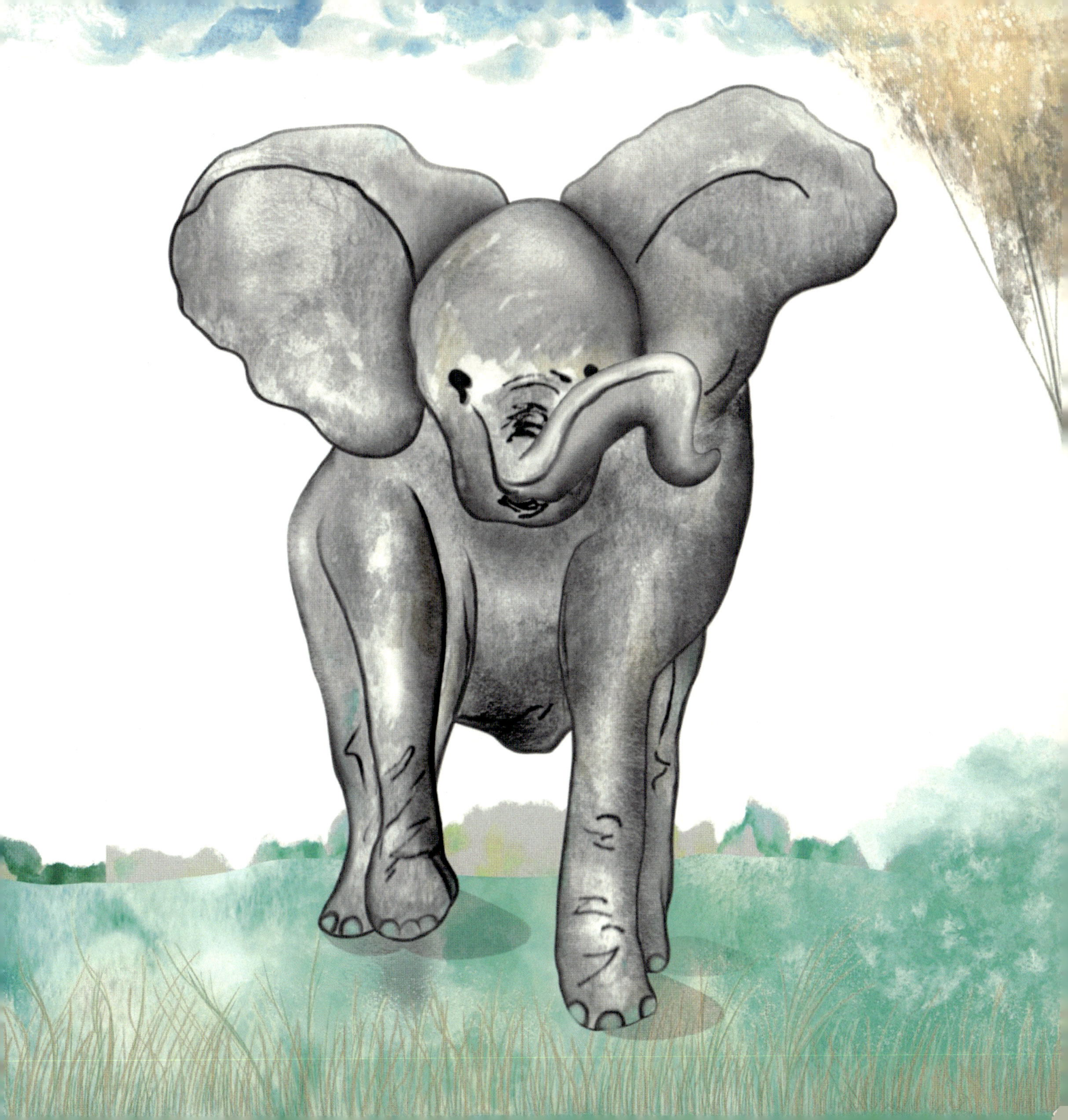

Pigs are sometimes pink,

and they do sometimes stink!

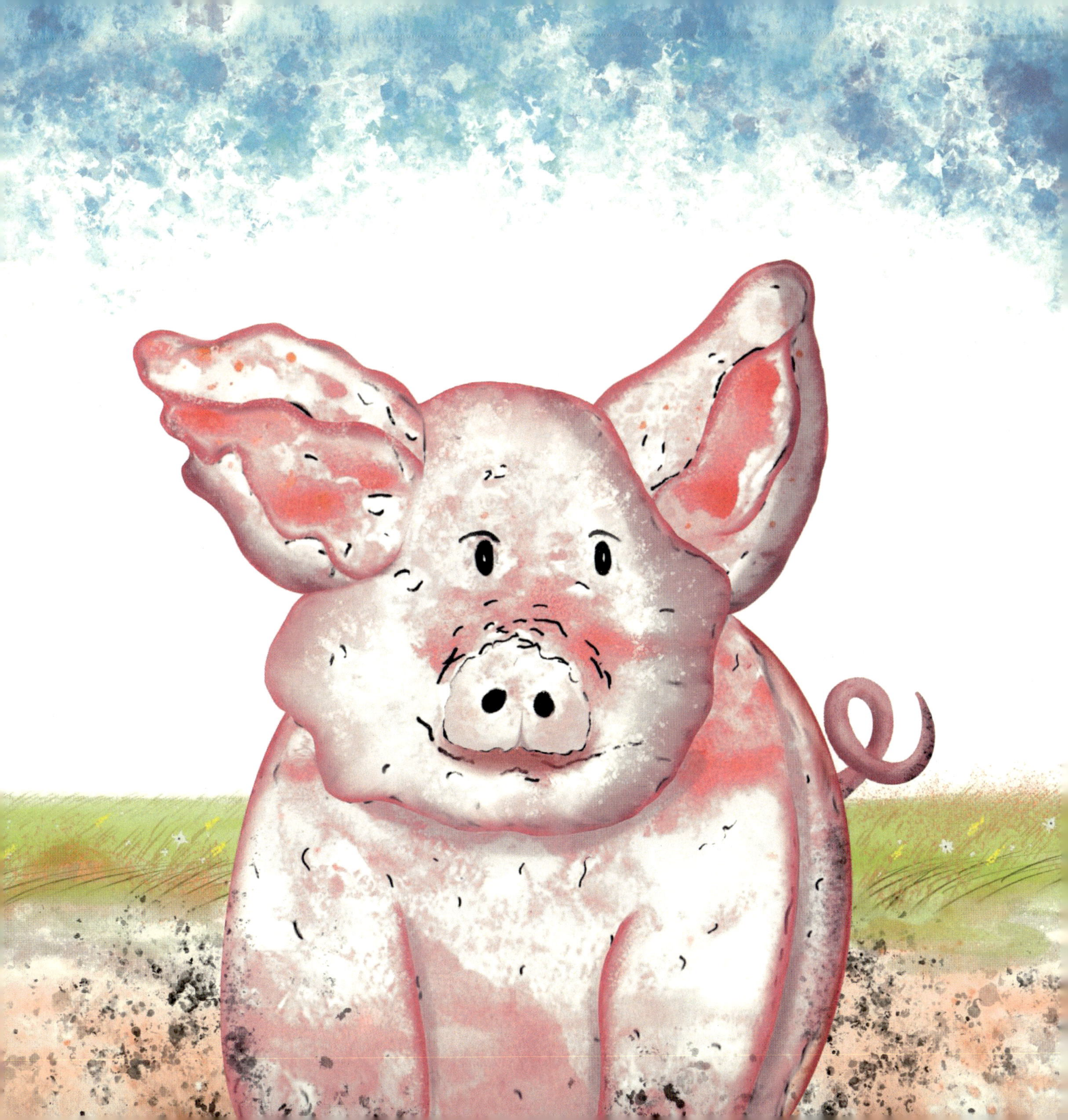

We saw a giraffe that was taller
than a house,

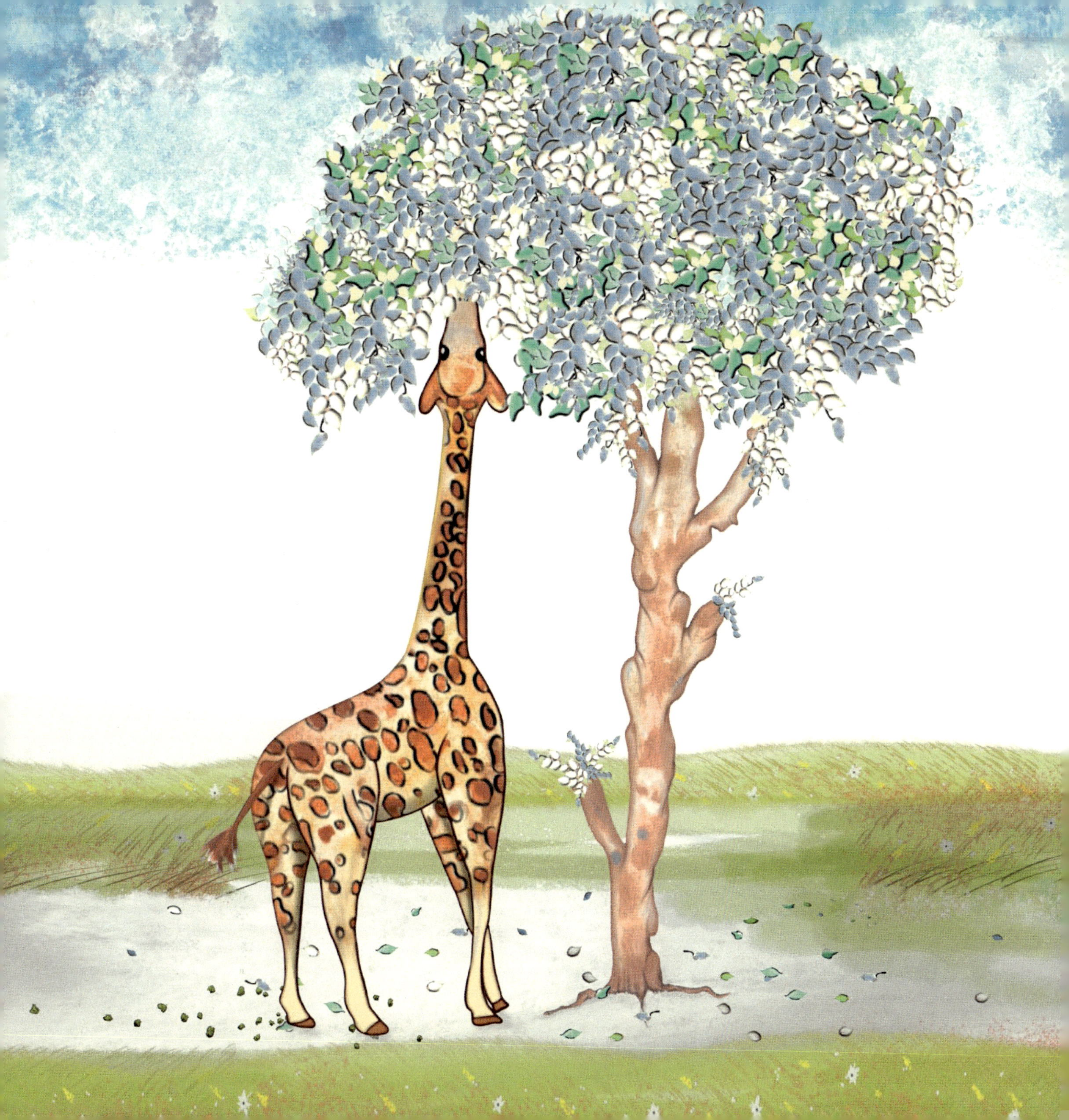

then we saw a bird that was smaller than a mouse.

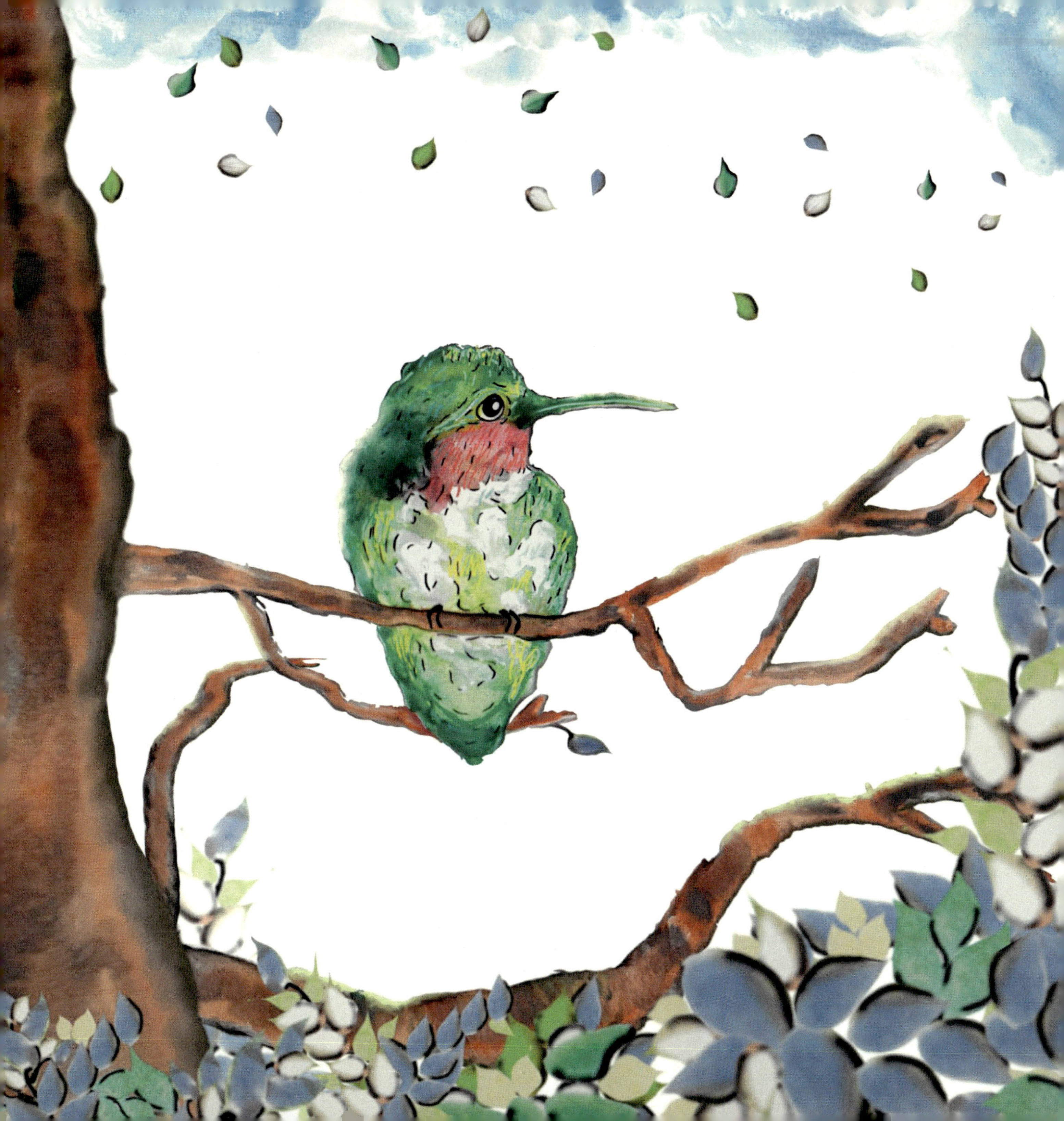

We saw some bats

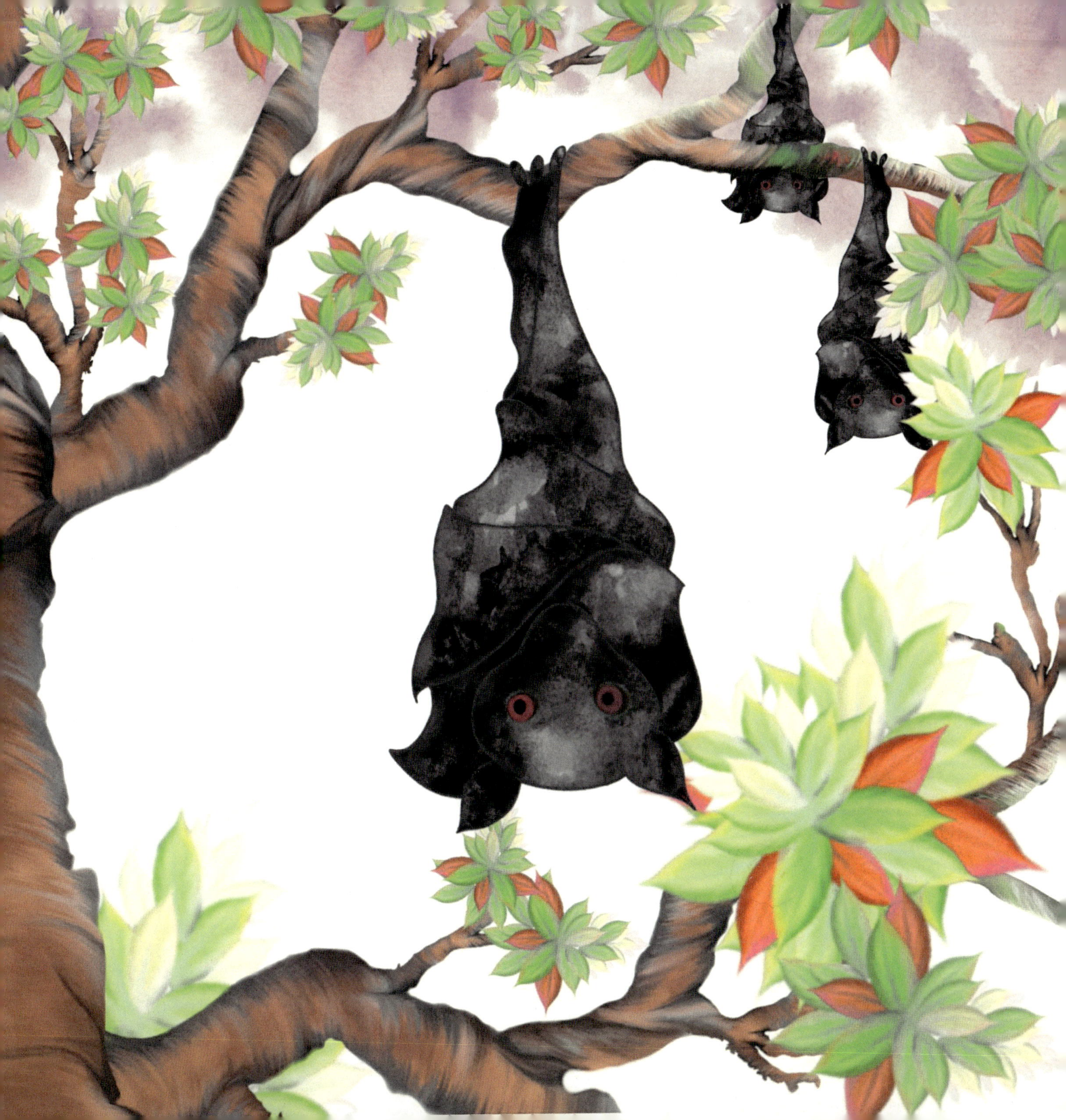

and a lot of different cats.

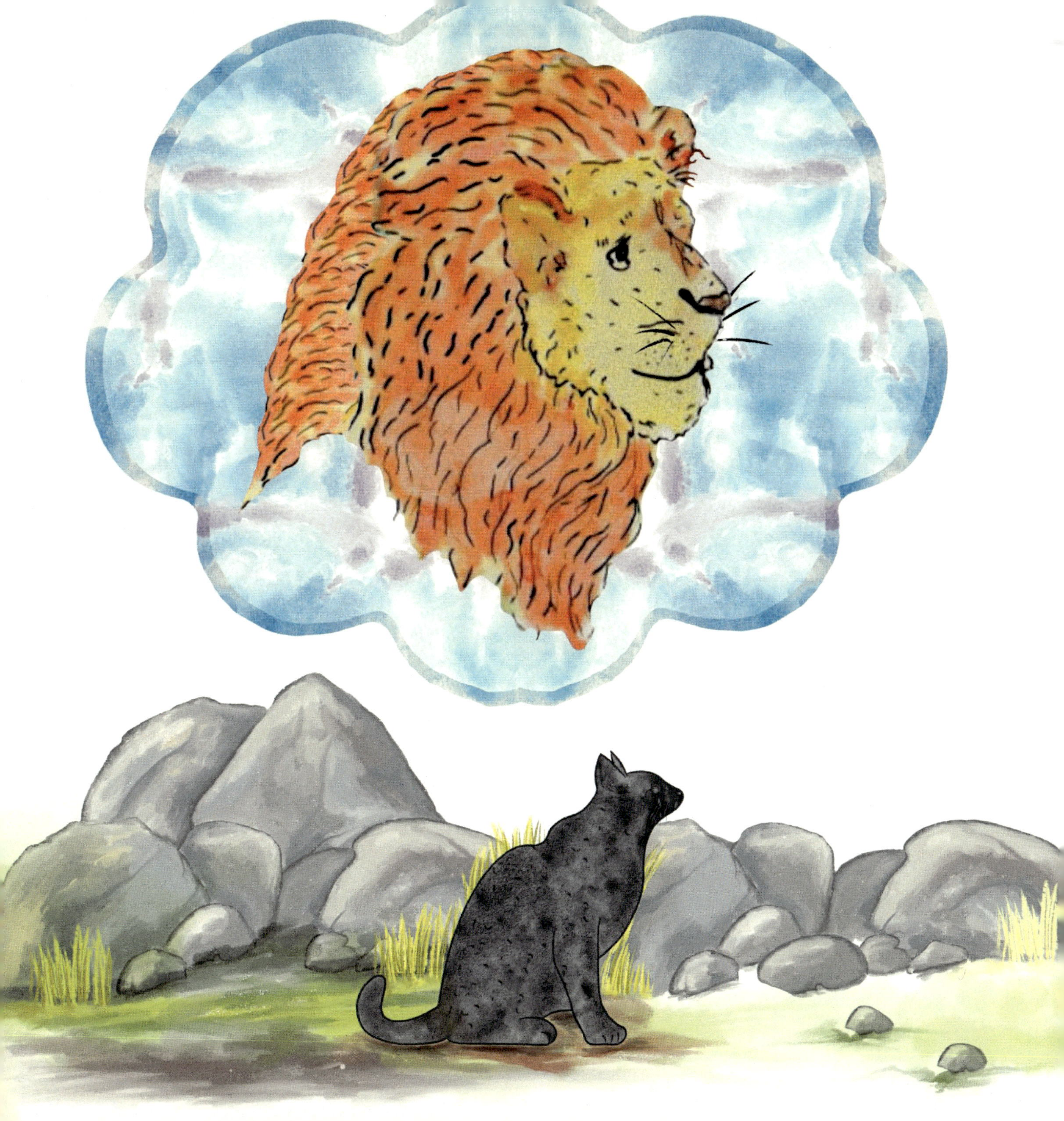

My family loved the dolphin show,

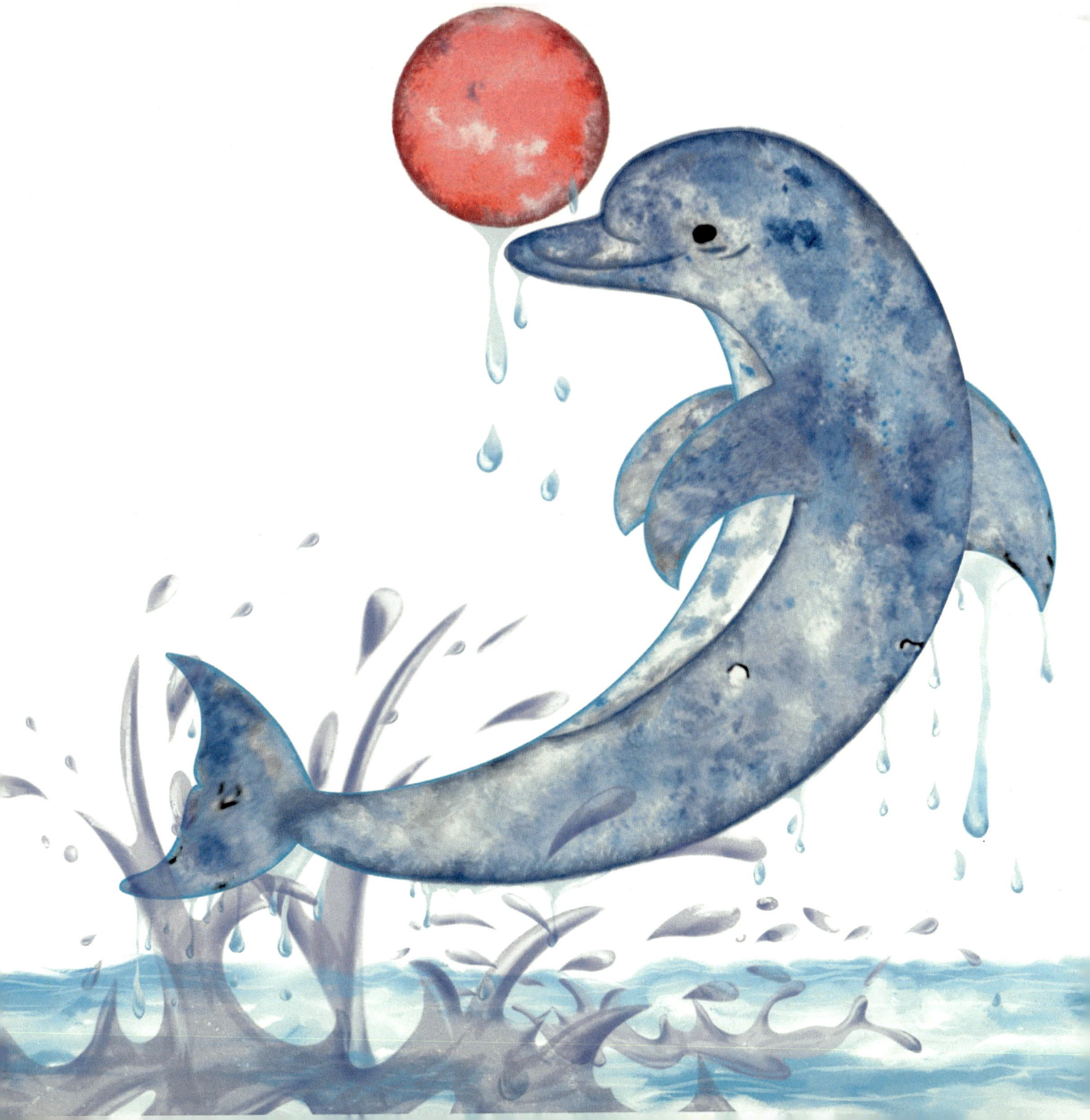

then next door to see moon jellyfish glow.

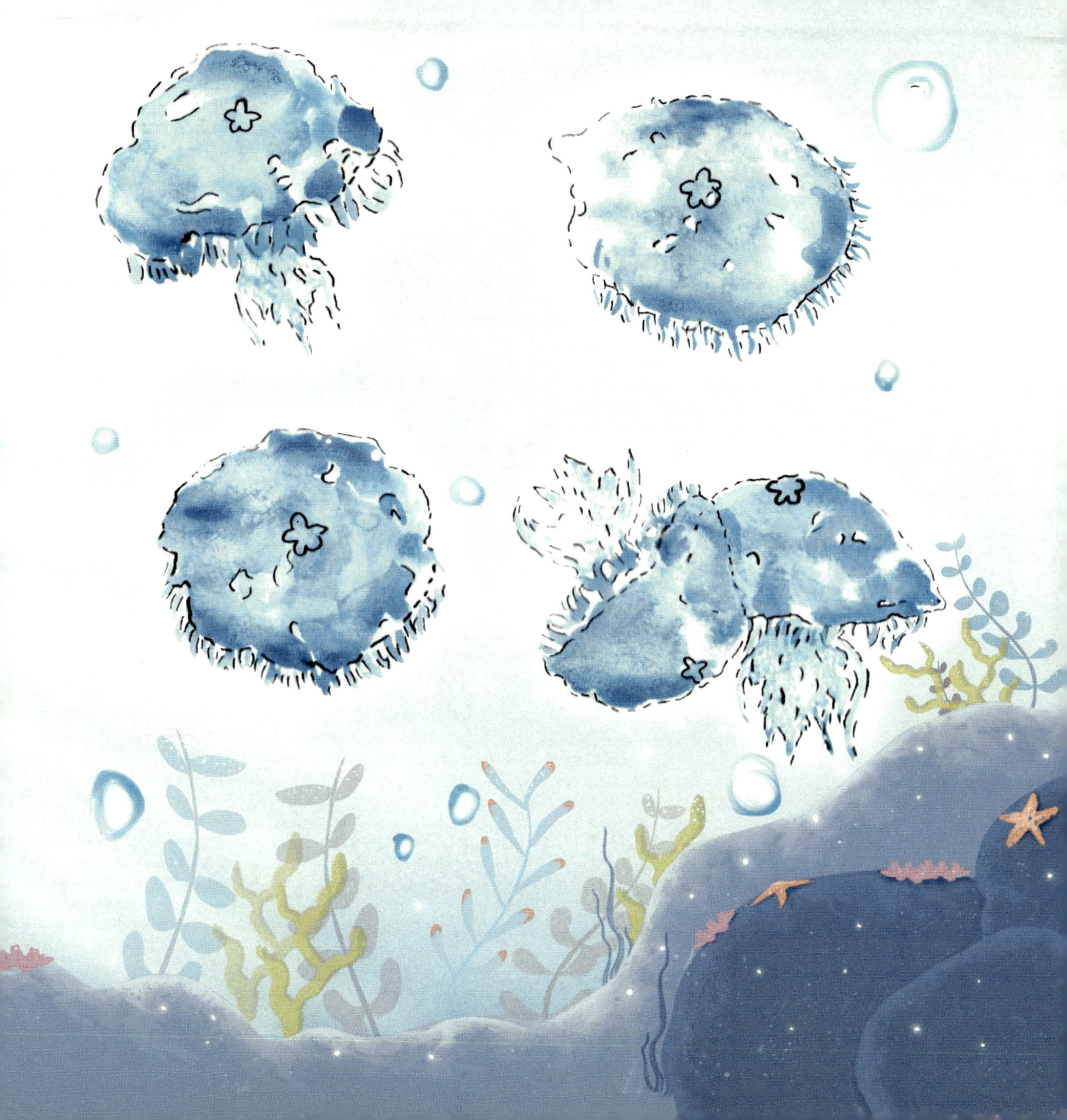

Penguins waddle and mate for life,
and their feathers are black and white.

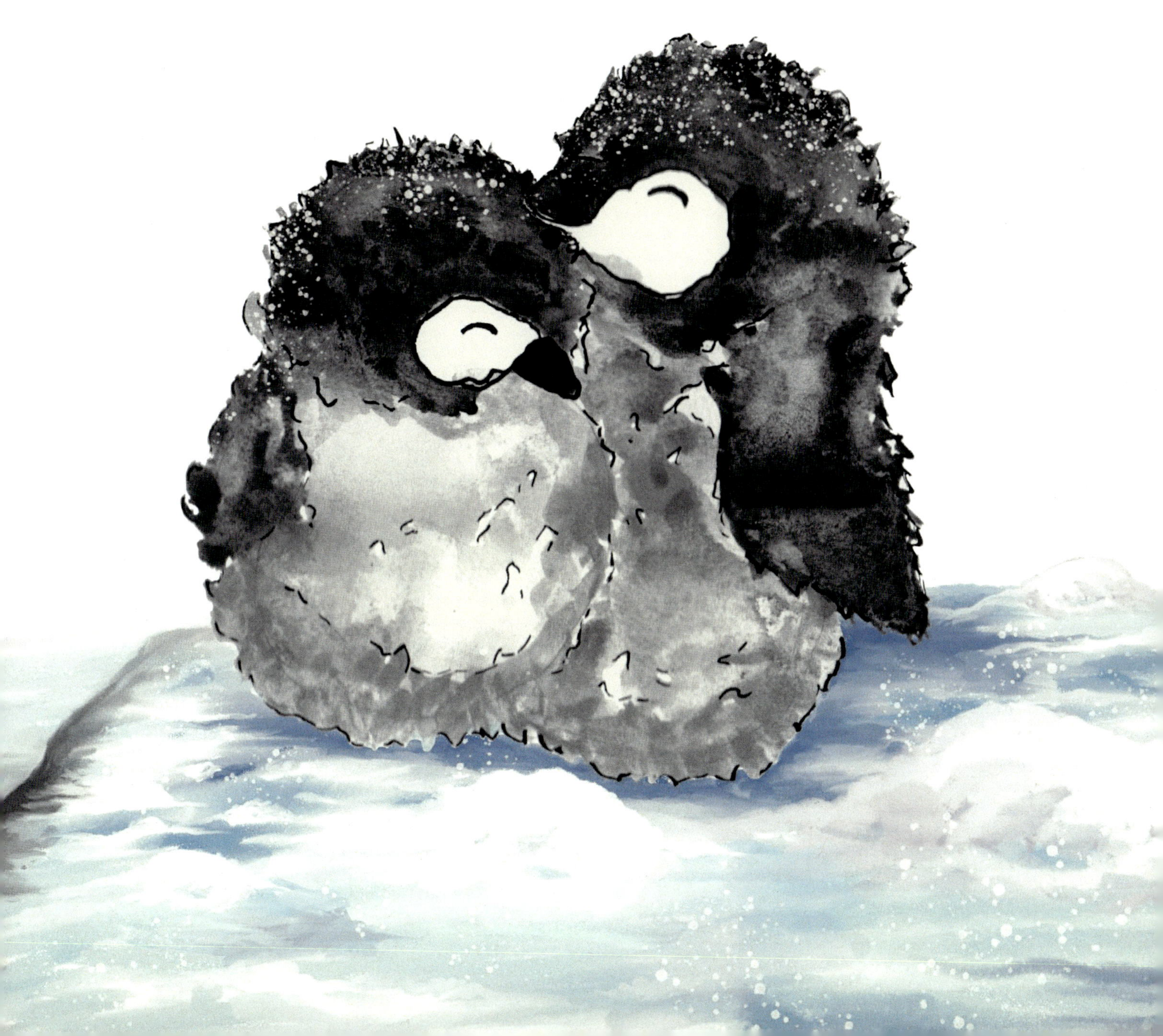

There is an animal that isn't quite nice,
its teeth are sharp and cut like knives.

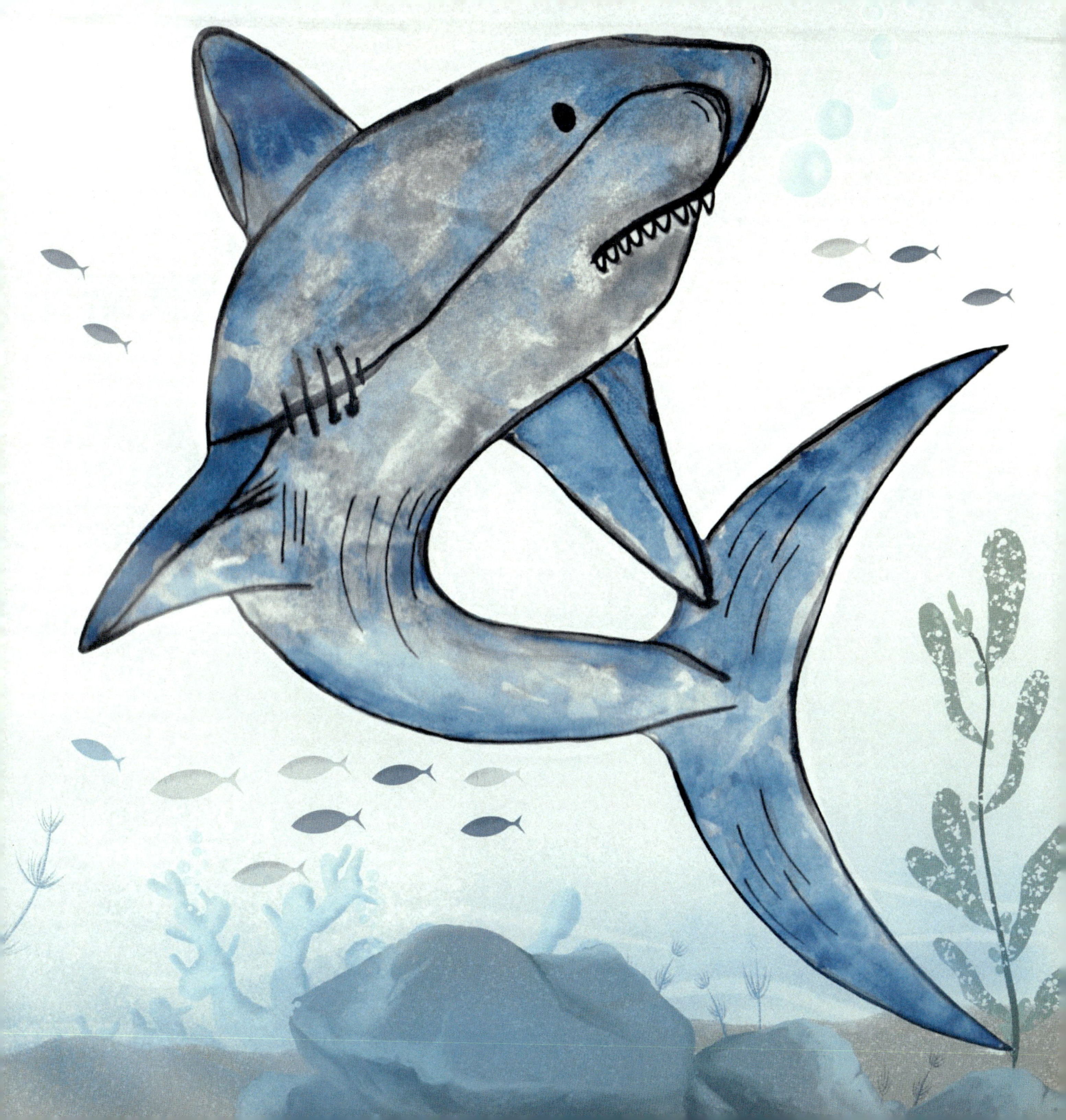

We saw some itty-bitty mice

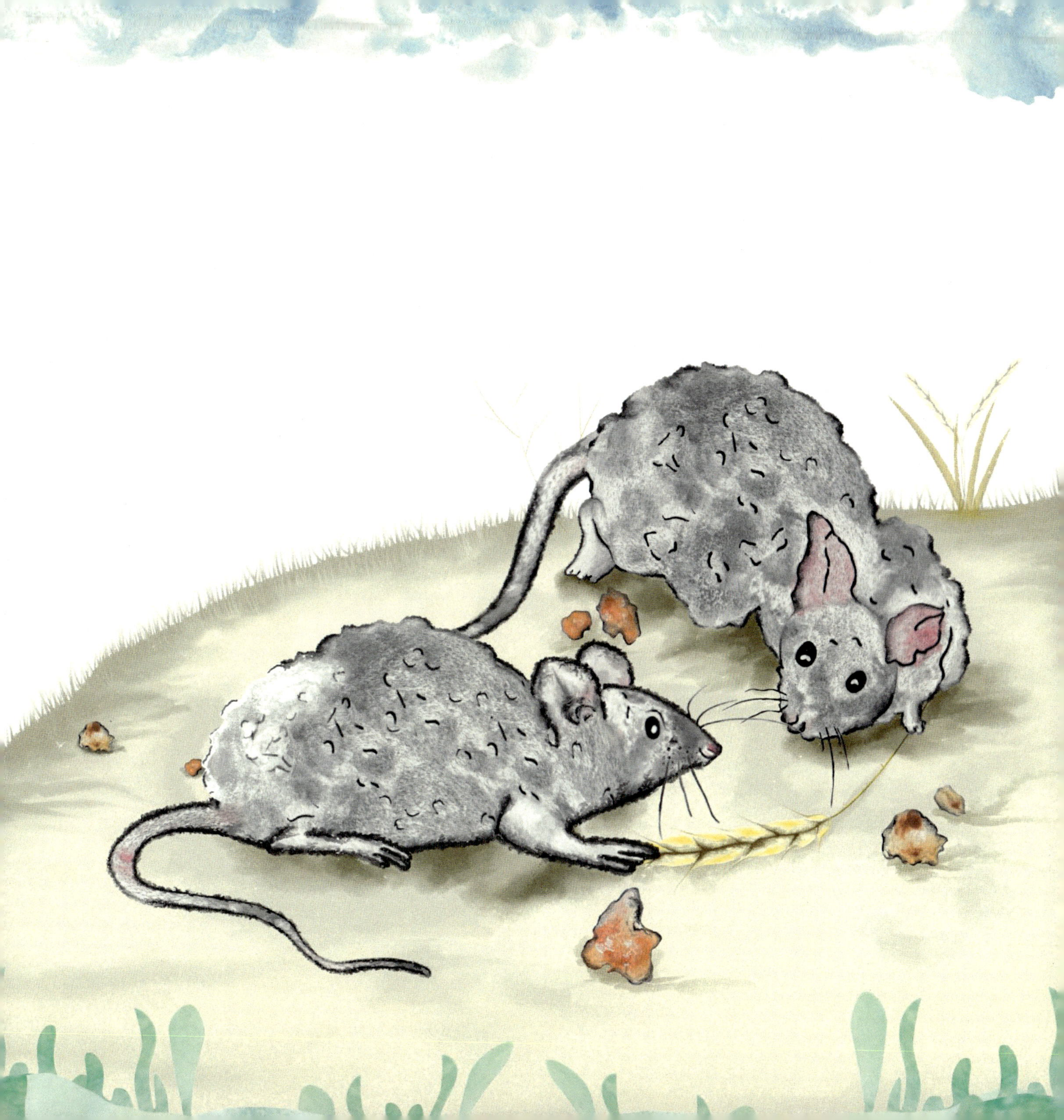

and an animal that prefers freezing ice.

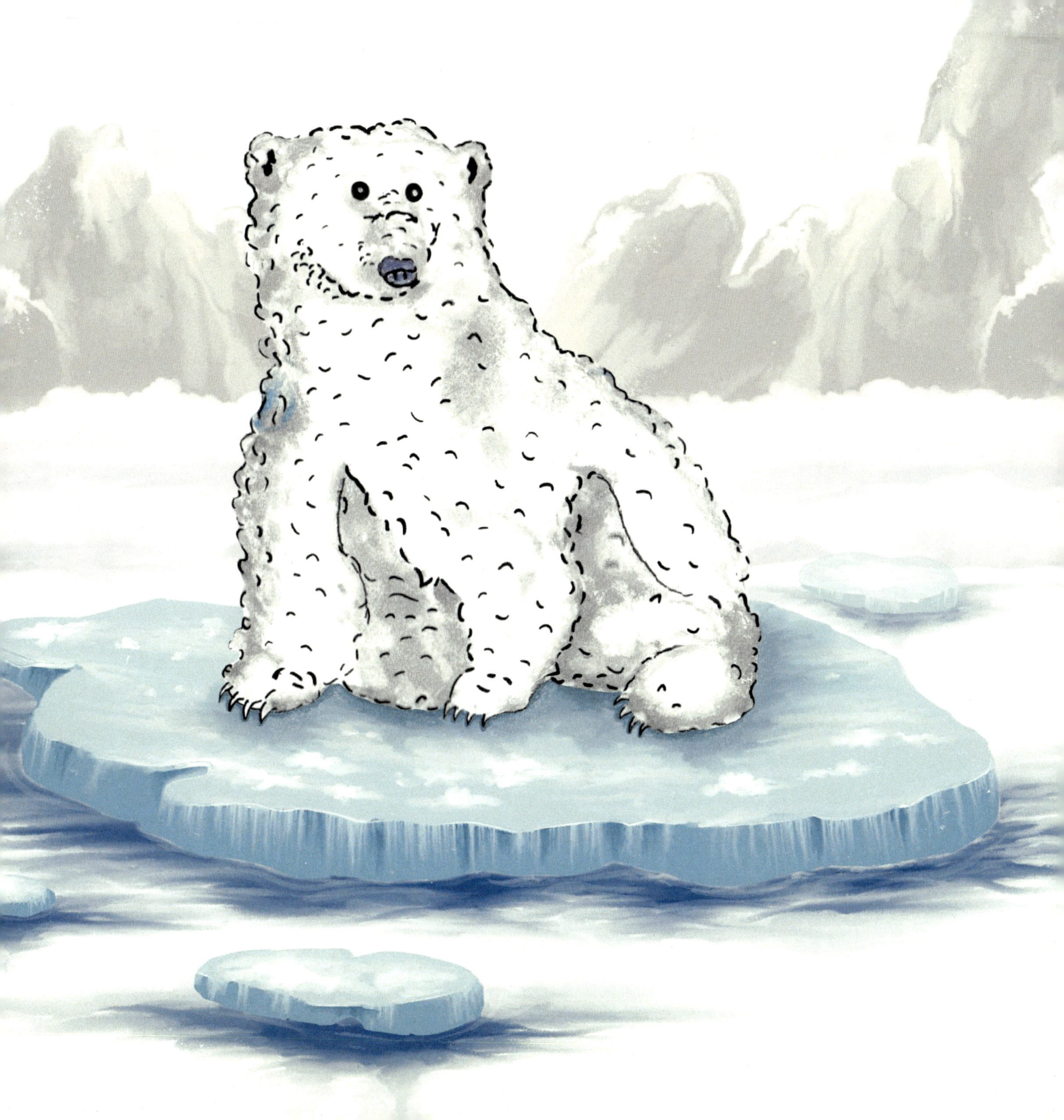

Our day at the zoo was fun and new.
Although I was sad to pack up and go,
I promised to keep the zoo in my heart
wherever I go!

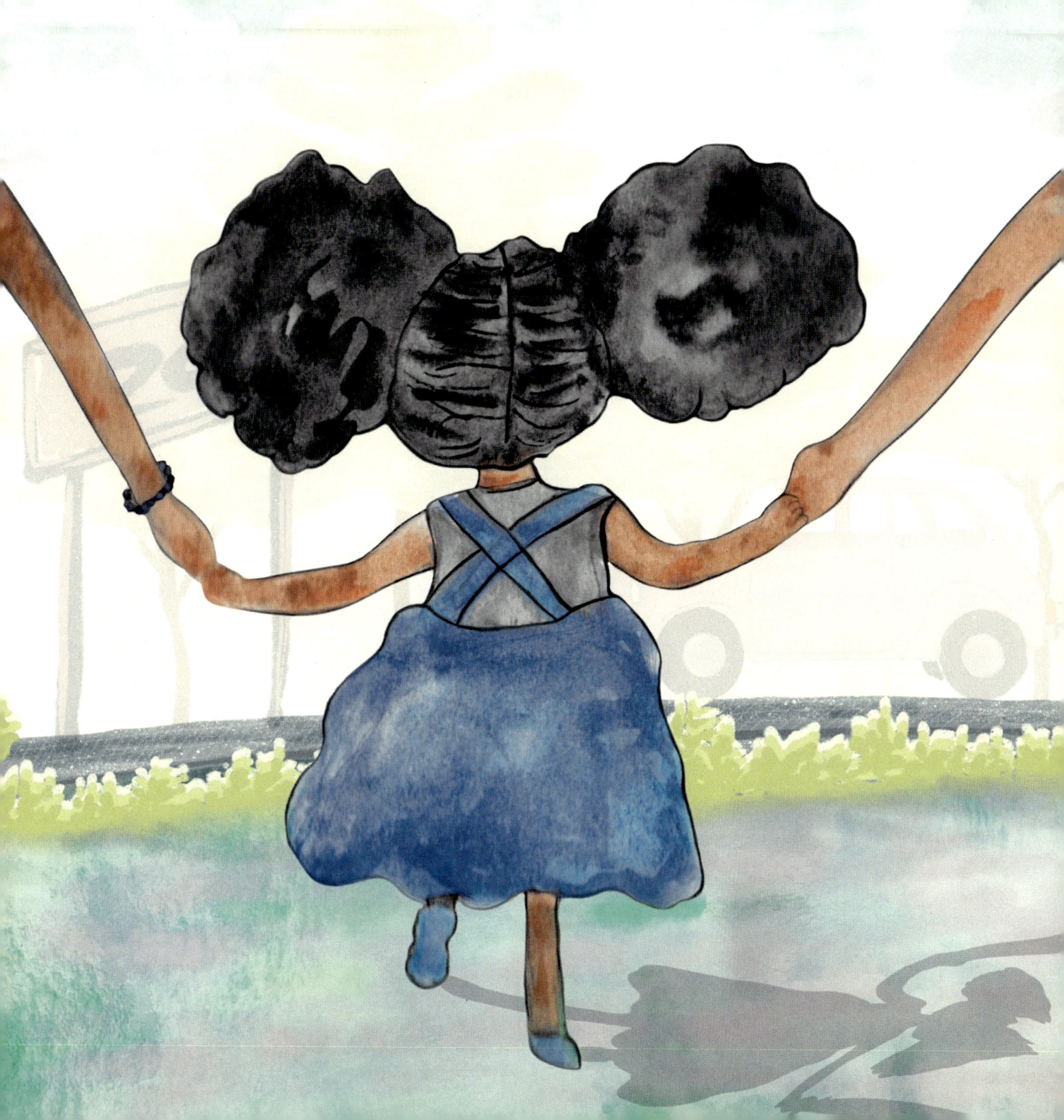

From a very young age I have had an intense infinity for all living things. I want my voice to reach all people so we can speak for those in nature that do not have one. Our environment needs strong individuals that want to stand up and make a change! You are the one. Your voice makes a difference and it all starts in the classroom, by educating yourself and others on conservation and environmental issues. You are teaching yourself that what you do makes a difference. This allows you to have the courage to speak out and make a change.

♥Disclaimer: Not all sharks are unkind! In fact, they are a interictal part of our ocean's ecosystems and play an important role in the health of the ocean.

WORLD

CREW

CLEAN-UP

I pledge to be a part of the world clean-up crew and make small daily efforts to help to take care of our living world.

Signed _____

Officiated _Gabriella Fabiano_

Made in the USA
Monee, IL
18 February 2022